Don't Be Sad, Sam

It's OK

Lisa Regan

Enslow Publishing

101 W. 23rd Street
Suite 240
New York, NY 10011
USA

enslow.com

It might be useful for parents or teachers to read our "How to use this book" guide on pages 28–29 before looking at Sam's dilemmas. The points for discussion on these pages are helpful to share with your child once you have read the book together.

This edition published in 2018 by Enslow Publishing, LLC.
101 W. 23rd Street, Suite 240, New York, NY 10011

Cataloging-in-Publication Data

Names: Regan, Lisa.
Title: Don't be sad, Sam: it's ok / Lisa Regan.
Description: New York : Enslow Publishing, 2018. |
 Series: You choose | Includes index.
Identifiers: ISBN 9780766088832 (pbk.) |
 ISBN 9780766086982 (library bound) |
 ISBN 9780766088795 (6 pack)
Subjects: LCSH: Sadness—Juvenile literature. |
 Emotions—Juvenile literature.
Classification: LCC BF723.S15 R44 2018 | DDC 152.4—dc23

Printed in the United States of America

Illustrations by Lucy Neale

Contents

Hello, Sam!

Like other children, Sam sometimes gets **sad**. He doesn't want to be **unhappy**. But now and then sad things happen that make Sam want to **cry**.

Follow Sam as he finds himself in situations in which he feels **sad**.

YOU Choose too!

Be brave, Sam

Oh, no! Sam drops a plate while helping Dad with the washing up.

The plate smashes into
pieces on the ground.
Dad looks really **upset**
and a little bit **angry**.

What should Sam choose to do?

Should Sam:

a shut himself in his bedroom?

b say sorry to Dad and help to pick up the pieces (then have a cuddle)?

c curl into a
ball and cry?

Sam, choose **b**

Grown-ups **understand** that **accidents** happen. If they are upset, it is because of the accident, not because of you. If they seem angry, try to remember that they are not angry at you.

What would YOU choose to do?

You can cry, Sam

Sam's pet **hamster** has **died**.

He knows that hamsters
don't live as long as people,
but he still feels like **crying**.

What should
Sam choose
to do?

Should Sam:

a stay awake all night **sobbing**?

b sit on his own and **refuse** to play with anyone?

C have a little cry and a big cuddle with Mom?

Sam, choose **C**

It's normal to feel sad when someone or something dies. Crying lets other people know that you are sad— then they can help you. After you've had a good cry, dry your tears and remember the good times.

What would YOU choose to do?

13

Stay friends, Sam

Sam's best friend Jonas is moving to a different town.

Sam doesn't want
Jonas to go away.

What should
Sam choose
to do?

Should Sam:

a plan to talk to Jonas on the computer after he moves?

b stop talking to his friend?

c say he has a tummy ache and can't go to school so he doesn't have to see Jonas?

Sam, choose **a**

It's okay to feel **upset** when someone goes away. You have to try harder to stay friends with people you don't see every day. Play with your other friends to help cheer you up, and make sure you keep in touch with the people who have moved away.

What would **YOU** **choose** to do?

Join in, Sam

Sam is watching his **classmates** in the playground.

He feels **left out** of their game.

What should Sam choose to do?

Should Sam:

a sit behind a tree away from all of the children?

b lock himself in the bathroom and feel sad?

C ask if he can join in with the others?

Sam, choose **C**

No one wants to feel left out. But usually people aren't trying to leave you out, they're just getting on with their game. Be **brave** and let them know that you want to join in.

What would YOU choose to do?

Speak up, Sam

Sam thinks his parents **love** his sister more than him.

It seems like they always do things with her.

What should Sam choose to do?

Should Sam:

a pack his bags to run away from home?

b ask his dad if they can do something fun together?

c stop talking to his mom and dad?

Sam, choose **b**

Don't ever feel sad by yourself. **Explain** how you feel to the person who is making you sad. Once they know what is wrong, they can try to help.

What would YOU **choose** to do?

25

Well done, Sam!

Hey, look at Sam! Now that he knows what to do, he's feeling much **happier**.

Did you choose the right thing to do? If you did, big cheers for you!

If you chose some of the other answers, try to think about Sam's choices so you can stop yourself from feeling too sad next time. Then it will be big smiles before long!

And remember— it's okay to feel sad for a while because things will get better soon.

How to use this book

This book can be used by an adult and a child together. It is based on common situations that can affect any child. Invite your child to talk about each of the choices. Ask questions such as "Why do you think Sam should talk to someone when he feels sad?"

Discuss the wrong choices, as well as the right ones, with your child. Describe what is happening in the following pictures and talk about what the wrong and right choices might be.

• Don't be scared to tell someone you're sad. They can't help you to feel better if they don't know how you feel.

• Running away doesn't ever help. You may still feel sad inside, even if you are far away from whatever is making you sad.

• Crying helps bad feelings to come out and helps you to feel better.

• Try not to feel sad for too long. Crying for a very long time can just make you feel worse.

Ask your child to tell you what makes them feel sad. Discuss things that make you feel upset, and tell them how you feel inside. Explain that it's okay to have these feelings, and that it happens to just about everyone.

Encourage your child to talk about their feelings rather than keeping them secret. Ask them if crying helps, and if they feel like they need a cuddle. Help your child to learn what makes them feel better, and which people they trust to talk to about how they are feeling. Let your child know that it's fine to feel sad sometimes, but that it is important to have fun times, too!

Glossary

accidents Things that happen
without you meaning them to, such
as breaking a plate or falling over.

brave Feeling strong enough to
do something that seems scary.

classmates Children in your class.

explain To show how something works.

hamster A small, furry animal that
is kept as a pet.

refuse To not do something when asked.

sobbing Crying so hard that it hurts.

understand To know something.

unhappy Feeling sad.

upset Feeling sad or mad.

Index

Titles in the series

Like all children, Annie sometimes gets really, really angry! She has lots of choices to make—but which are the CALM ones?

Like all children, Carlos sometimes does things that are wrong and doesn't come clean. He has lots of choices to make—but which are the TRUTHFUL ones?

Like all children, Charlie sometimes feels a little scared. He has lots of choices to make—but which are the BRAVE ones?

Like all children, Gertie sometimes plays a little dirty. She has lots of choices to make—but which are the FAIR ones?

Like all children, Harry sometimes takes things that don't belong to him. He has lots of choices to make—but which are the HONEST ones?

Like all children, Henry sometimes gets angry and sometimes he hits, too. He has lots of choices to make—but which are the GENTLE ones?

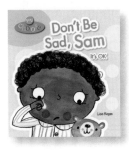

Like all children, Sam sometimes feels sad, and he doesn't know how to make himself feel better. He has lots of choices to make—but which are the HAPPY ones?

Like all children, Tilly wants to do everything *right now*, and sometimes she just can't wait! She has lots of choices to make—but which are the PATIENT ones?